Success With

Grammar

SCHOLASTIC

Editor: Ourania Papacharalambous
Cover design by Tannaz Fassihi; cover illustration by Kevin Zimmer
Interior design by Mina Chen
Interior illustrations by Gabriele Tafuni (3)
Photos ©: JKendall/Getty Images (34); all other photos © Shutterstock.com

ISBN 978-1-338-79841-8
Scholastic Inc., 557 Broadway, New York, NY 10012
Copyright © 2022 Scholastic Inc.
All rights reserved. Printed in the U.S.A.
First printing, January 2022
1 2 3 4 5 6 7 8 9 10   40 29 28 27 26 25 24 23 22

INTRODUCTION

No other resource boosts grammar skills like *Scholastic Success With Grammar*! For classroom or at-home use, this exciting series for grades 1 through 5 provides invaluable reinforcement and practice in grammar topics such as sentence types, verb tenses, parts of speech, subject-verb agreement, common and proper nouns, punctuation, sentence structure, capitalization, and more!

This 48-page book contains loads of clever practice pages to keep kids challenged and excited as they strengthen the grammar skills they need to read and write well. On page 4, you will find a list of the key skills covered in the activities throughout this book. Each practice page reinforces a specific, age-appropriate skill. What's more, the activities for each skill are followed by an assessment sheet that gives students realistic practice in taking tests—and gives you a useful tool to follow their progress!

Take the lead and help students succeed with *Scholastic Success With Grammar*. Parents and teachers agree: No one helps students succeed like Scholastic.

TABLE OF CONTENTS

Key Skills 4

Types of Sentences 5

Simple and Complete Subjects
    and Predicates 8

Compound Subjects and Predicates 11

Compound Sentences 14

Common and Proper Nouns 17

Singular and Plural Nouns 20

Subject and Object Pronouns 23

Possessive Pronouns 26

Action Verbs 29

Verb Tenses and Agreement 32

Main and Helping Verbs 35

Linking Verbs 38

Irregular Verbs 41

Adjectives 44

Answer Key 47

Grade-Appropriate Skills Covered in
Scholastic Success With Grammar: Grade 4

Know and apply grade-level phonics and word analysis skills in decoding words.

Read with sufficient accuracy and fluency to support comprehension.

Demonstrate command of the conventions of standard English grammar and usage when writing or speaking.

Use relative pronouns and relative adverbs.

Order adjectives within sentences according to conventional patterns.

Form and use prepositional phrases.

Produce complete sentences, recognizing and correcting inappropriate fragments and run-ons.

Correctly use frequently confused words.

Demonstrate command of the conventions of standard English capitalization, punctuation, and spelling when writing.

Use correct capitalization.

Use commas and quotation marks to mark direct speech and quotations from a text.

Use a comma before a coordinating conjunction in a compound sentence.

Spell grade-appropriate words correctly, consulting references as needed.

Use knowledge of language and its conventions when writing, speaking, reading, or listening.

Choose words and phrases to convey ideas precisely.

Choose punctuation for effect.

Types of Sentences

What kind of sentence is each of the following? Write *declarative, interrogative, exclamatory,* or *imperative* on the line.

A **declarative sentence** makes a statement. An **interrogative sentence** asks a question. An **exclamatory sentence** shows strong feeling. An **imperative sentence** states a command.

1. Merlin carried the baby to safety. _____

2. Slip the sword into the groove, and pull it out. _____

3. The king was England's bravest ruler! _____

4. Who will follow Selene? _____

Identify which groups of words are incomplete sentences and which are complete sentences. Write *incomplete* or *complete* on the line.

1. Sarah at the edge of the square. _____

2. The knights fought so bravely! _____

3. How did Kay treat her dog? _____

4. The sword out of the stone. _____

5. Natalie was trained to be a pilot. _____

Rewrite the incomplete sentences from the activity above. Add an action word to each.

1. _____

2. _____

Types of Sentences

Add the correct end punctuation mark to each sentence. Then, write *declarative*, *interrogative*, *exclamatory*, or *imperative* to tell what kind of sentence it is.

1 How do turtles protect themselves _____

2 What heavy, hot suits of steel they wore _____

3 Pretend that you are an acrobat or juggler _____

4 The students sang songs, told stories, and recited poems _____

Complete each sentence below with your own verb. Then, identify each sentence by writing *declarative*, *interrogative*, *exclamatory*, or *imperative*.

1 The audience _____ to the band. _____

2 What kind of games did pioneers like to _____? _____

3 Please _____ the pepper. _____

4 I _____ three chess games in a row! _____

Choose two types of sentences (declarative, interrogative, exclamatory, or imperative). Write an example for each type below. Then, circle the type of sentence you wrote.

1 _____

declarative   interrogative   exclamatory   imperative

2 _____

declarative   interrogative   exclamatory   imperative

Types of Sentences

Decide if there is an error in the underlined part of each sentence.
Fill in the bubble next to the correct answer.

1 <u>you do like</u> to watch movies about knights and castles?
- ○ You do like
- ○ Do you like
- ○ correct as is

2 Please hand me that mystery book about <u>the Middle Ages?</u>
- ○ the Middle Ages!
- ○ the Middle Ages.
- ○ correct as is

3 Grandfather described life in the early part <u>of the century.</u>
- ○ of the century?
- ○ of the century!
- ○ correct as is

4 Why don't you write about <u>your life!</u>
- ○ your life?
- ○ your life.
- ○ correct as is

5 <u>Begin by describing</u> your very first memory.
- ○ begin by describing
- ○ By describing
- ○ correct as is

6 I had such fun swimming <u>in the ocean?</u>
- ○ in the ocean
- ○ in the ocean!
- ○ correct as is

7 What do you remember about your first day <u>in school?</u>
- ○ in school!
- ○ in school.
- ○ correct as is

8 <u>another story</u> about our relatives in Mexico.
- ○ Tell me another story
- ○ Another story
- ○ correct as is

9 The fish looked so colorful swimming in <u>the Caribbean Sea</u>
- ○ the Caribbean Sea!
- ○ the Caribbean Sea?
- ○ correct as is

10 He told us about <u>his trip?</u>
- ○ his trip
- ○ his trip.
- ○ correct as is

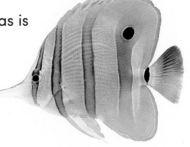

Simple and Complete Subjects and Predicates

> The **simple subject** is the main noun or pronoun that tells whom or what the sentence is about. The **complete subject** is the simple subject and all of the words that go with it. The **simple predicate** is the verb that tells what the subject does or is. The **complete predicate** is the verb and all the words that tell what the subject does or is.

Draw a line between the complete subject and the complete predicate. Underline the complete subject once and the simple subject twice.

1 A small family lived on a faraway planet.

2 The family's two children played near the space launch.

3 The little girl dreamed about life on Earth.

4 Huge spaceships landed daily on the planet.

Draw a line between the complete subject and the complete predicate. Underline the complete predicate once and the simple predicate twice.

1 The planet's inhabitants lived in underground homes.

2 A special machine manufactures air inside the family's home.

3 Many toys and games cluttered the children's playroom.

4 The children's father described weather on Earth.

Circle the complete subject in each sentence. Underline the complete predicate.

1 The underground home contained large, comfortable rooms.

2 The playful child rolled his clay into a ball.

Simple and Complete Subjects and Predicates

Read each sentence. Circle the complete subject. Underline the simple subject.

1 My whole family had a picnic on Saturday.

2 The warm, sunny day was perfect for an outing in the park.

3 My cousin Fred brought his guitar and harmonica.

4 Everyone sang favorite folk songs.

Read each sentence. Circle the complete predicate. Underline the simple predicate.

1 We watched the space shuttle on TV this morning.

2 The huge spaceship rocketed into space at 6:00 A.M.

3 During the flight, the six astronauts released a satellite into space.

4 The spacecraft landed smoothly on Monday at noon.

Write two sentences. Circle the complete subject and underline the complete predicate in each sentence.

1 _____

_____

2 _____

_____

Simple and Complete Subjects and Predicates

What part of each sentence is underlined? Fill in the bubble next to the correct answer.

1 <u>My cousin</u> lives on a big ranch in Montana.
- ○ simple subject
- ○ complete subject
- ○ simple predicate

2 Her family <u>raises cattle on the ranch</u>.
- ○ complete subject
- ○ simple predicate
- ○ complete predicate

3 Rosa's <u>job</u> is feeding the chickens before school.
- ○ simple subject
- ○ complete subject
- ○ simple predicate

4 Her brother John <u>feeds the horses</u>.
- ○ complete subject
- ○ simple predicate
- ○ complete predicate

5 <u>My cousin Rosa</u> rides her horse across the range.
- ○ simple subject
- ○ complete subject
- ○ complete predicate

6 John <u>spreads</u> fresh hay in the pasture.
- ○ simple subject
- ○ simple predicate
- ○ complete predicate

7 Their nearest <u>neighbors</u> often go into town with them.
- ○ simple subject
- ○ complete subject
- ○ simple predicate

8 The dinner bell <u>rings</u> at 6:30 every evening.
- ○ simple subject
- ○ complete subject
- ○ simple predicate

9 <u>The whole family</u> sits on the porch and reads about space.
- ○ simple subject
- ○ complete subject
- ○ complete predicate

10 Rosa <u>uses her laptop to research animals</u>.
- ○ complete subject
- ○ simple predicate
- ○ complete predicate

Compound Subjects and Predicates

A **compound subject** is two or more subjects in the same sentence, usually joined by a connecting word such as *and* or *or*. A **compound predicate** is two or more verbs in the same sentence, usually joined by a connecting word such as *and* or *or*.

Underline the compound subject in each sentence.

1. The bears, rabbits, and pigs attended a party.

2. Carrots, beets, and squash grow in the garden.

3. Later this month, Teddy and Osito will visit Baby Bear.

4. My brothers and sisters really enjoyed the housewarming.

Circle the compound predicate in each sentence.

1. Peter's mother cleaned and peeled the crispy carrots.

2. The guests laughed and giggled at June's funny jokes.

3. The sly wolves waited and watched for the passing animals.

4. Goldilocks weeds and waters her garden every day.

5. The author writes and edits her amusing fairy tales.

Write the compound subject or compound predicate that completes each sentence. Then, write *CS* for compound subject or *CP* for compound predicate.

authors and illustrators   buys and reads

1. My friend _____ all of that author's books. _____

2. Many _____ visit our school. _____

Compound Subjects and Predicates

Underline the simple subject in each sentence. Then, rewrite the two sentences as one sentence with a compound subject.

1 The teacher visited the ocean. Her students visited the ocean.

_____

2 Seagulls flew overhead. Pelicans flew overhead.

_____

3 Carlos ran on the beach. Tanya ran on the beach.

_____

4 Seashells littered the sand. Seaweed littered the sand.

_____

Circle the simple predicate in each sentence. Then, rewrite the two sentences as one sentence with a compound predicate.

1 The artist paints sea life. The artist draws sea life.

_____

2 I collect driftwood. I decorate driftwood.

_____

3 Seals swim near the pier. Seals dive near the pier.

_____

Compound Subjects and Predicates

Fill in the bubble next to the compound subject.

1 The deer and bison grazed in the high mountain meadow.
- ○ deer and bison
- ○ grazed in
- ○ high mountain meadow

2 Last weekend, Rosa and Kay camped by the lake.
- ○ Last weekend
- ○ Rosa and Kay
- ○ camped by

3 Last year, students and teachers created a wildlife mural.
- ○ Last year
- ○ wildlife mural
- ○ students and teachers

4 My friends and I were hiking in the White Mountains.
- ○ were hiking
- ○ friends and I
- ○ the White Mountains

Fill in the bubble next to the compound predicate.

1 All night long, the chilly wind moaned and howled.
- ○ All night long
- ○ chilly wind
- ○ moaned and howled

2 Joan picked and peeled the apples in the morning.
- ○ picked and peeled
- ○ the apples
- ○ in the morning

3 Many students wrote and revised their book reports.
- ○ Many students
- ○ wrote and revised
- ○ their book reports

4 The famous sculptor cut and polished the cold, gray granite.
- ○ famous sculptor
- ○ cut and polished
- ○ cold, gray granite

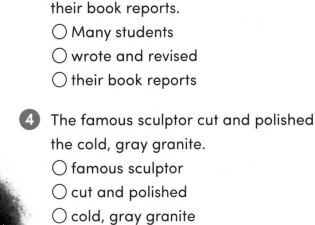

Compound Sentences

Read each sentence. Decide if it is a simple sentence or a compound sentence.
Write *simple* or *compound* on the line.

> A **compound sentence** joins two simple sentences with a comma and a **coordinating conjunction**. *And, but,* and *or* are common coordinating conjunctions.

1. Dad had been horseback riding before. _____

2. Paul felt a little nervous on a horse, but he would never admit it. _____

3. He discovered that riding was a lot of fun, and he couldn't wait to tell his friends about it. _____

4. There don't seem to be many bears in the national park this year. _____

5. Suddenly, Mom pointed out the car window toward some trees. _____

Underline the simple sentences that make up each compound sentence.

1. Connor had seen many parks in his life, but he never had seen a park like this one.

2. Dad brought a pair of binoculars, and Nate used them to look for animals.

3. He saw his first live bear, and the hair stood up on his arms.

4. It was an exciting moment, but it only lasted a second.

5. The bear was no bear at all, and Nate was embarrassed.

6. He hadn't seen a bear, but he kept looking.

Compound Sentences

Read each sentence. Underline the simple sentences that make up the compound sentence. Circle the coordinating conjunction in each sentence.

1 One day we were in the park, and we saw two ducks swimming by.

2 We watched the ducks for a while, but they disappeared into the tall grass.

3 The ducks might have gone to a nest, or they could have swum to the shore.

4 We walked along the grassy bank, but we could not find them anywhere.

5 We sat down on the dock, and out came the ducks again.

Read each compound sentence. Choose the coordinating conjunction that makes sense and write it on the line.

1 The ducklings are brown, _____ the adult ducks are white. (but, or)

2 The ducklings were playing, _____ they were learning, too. (but, or)

3 The ducklings ate a lot, _____ they grew quickly. (but, and)

4 We brought bread with us, _____ we fed the ducks. (and, but)

5 Maybe they liked us, _____ maybe they just liked the food. (and, or)

Write a compound sentence. Underline the simple sentences and circle the coordinating conjunction you used.

_____

_____

Compound Sentences

Fill in the bubble that tells whether the sentence is a simple sentence or a compound sentence.

1 There are many planets in our solar system, but there is only one sun.
○ simple
○ compound

2 The sun is a star, and a star is a giant ball of burning gases.
○ simple
○ compound

3 A moon is a satellite that moves around a planet.
○ simple
○ compound

4 Earth has only one moon, but the planet Mars has two moons.
○ simple
○ compound

Is the underlined part correct? Fill in the bubble next to the right answer.

1 The sun is <u>a star, but it is not</u> the biggest star.
○ a star but it is not
○ a star but, it is not
○ correct as is

2 Some stars are bigger than <u>the sun and, some stars</u> are smaller.
○ the sun and some stars
○ the sun, and some stars
○ correct as is

3 Other stars seem smaller than <u>the sun, they are</u> just farther away.
○ the sun, but they are
○ the sun, They are
○ correct as is

4 Do hot stars give off <u>blue light or do they</u> give off red light?
○ blue light or, do they
○ blue light, or do they
○ correct as is

Common and Proper Nouns

Circle the common nouns in each sentence.

1. The farmer lives in the green house down the road.

2. The farmer grows wheat, soybeans, and corn.

3. The fields are plowed before he plants the crop.

4. Crops are planted in rows so that they can be watered easily.

5. As the plants grow, the farmer removes weeds and looks for bugs.

Underline the proper nouns in each sentence.

1. John Vasquez grows soybeans and alfalfa on a 30-acre farm near Tulsa, Oklahoma.

2. The Vasquez Farm is next to the Rising J Horse Ranch.

3. Mr. Vasquez and his daughter Sally sell alfalfa to the owner of the ranch.

4. Sometimes Joker, a quarter horse, knocks down the fence to get the alfalfa.

5. Every October, people come to the Vasquez Farm for the annual Harvest Celebration.

Rewrite each sentence. Replace each underlined common noun with a proper noun.

1. We walked down the street to the park.

2. My aunt lives in the city.

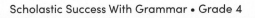

Common and Proper Nouns

Circle the common nouns in each sentence. Underline the proper nouns.

1 The *Atlanta Constitution* published a story about celebrations.

2 *Three Dogs on a Summer Night* is a movie about poodles.

3 We like to sing "She'll Be Comin' 'Round the Mountain" at the campfire.

4 Last August, my best friend, Josh, went to Germany with his grandparents.

5 My family always goes to the beach for Memorial Day.

Complete the chart below by writing each common and proper noun in the correct column. Then, add three common nouns and three proper nouns to the chart.

	Common Nouns	Proper Nouns
newspaper	newspaper	The Sun News
The Sun News		
day		
magazine		
July		
Harry Potter		
Yellowstone National Park		
National Geographic		
city		
book		
month		
Tuesday		
park		
Chicago		

Common and Proper Nouns

Read each sentence. Are the underlined nouns written correctly?
Fill in the bubble next to the right answer.

1 I go to <u>abraham lincoln school</u>.
- ○ abraham lincoln School
- ○ Abraham Lincoln School
- ○ correct as is

2 I brought <u>a peanut butter sandwich</u>.
- ○ a Peanut Butter sandwich
- ○ a peanut butter Sandwich
- ○ correct as is

3 I sang <u>row, row, row your boat</u> today.
- ○ Row, Row, Row Your Boat
- ○ "Row, Row, Row Your Boat"
- ○ correct as is

4 My school is located on the <u>corner of Maple Avenue and Elm Street</u>.
- ○ Corner of Maple Avenue and Elm Street
- ○ corner of Maple avenue and Elm street
- ○ correct as is

5 I wrote a book report on *<u>hello, universe</u>* for reading class.
- ○ *Hello, Universe*
- ○ *Hello, universe*
- ○ correct as is

6 <u>My best friend, John,</u> sits in the third row.
- ○ My Best Friend John
- ○ My best Friend John
- ○ correct as is

7 My <u>spanish class begins at noon</u>.
- ○ Spanish class begins at Noon
- ○ Spanish class begins at noon
- ○ correct as is

8 That painting <u>is called "Sunflowers."</u>
- ○ is Called sunflowers.
- ○ is called Sunflowers.
- ○ correct as is

9 I wrote about <u>washington, d.c.</u>
- ○ about Washington, D.C.
- ○ about Washington, d.c.
- ○ correct as is

10 Later I'll go to <u>austin's better books</u>.
- ○ Austin's Better Books
- ○ austin's Better Books
- ○ correct as is

Singular and Plural Nouns

A **singular noun** names one person, place, thing, or idea. A **plural noun** names more than one person, place, thing, animal, or idea. Add *-s* to form the plural of most nouns. Some plural nouns are irregular, and their spellings need to be memorized.

Underline the singular nouns in each sentence.

1 I opened the door and found the shoes, cap, and bat I needed for the game.

2 I headed down to the fields with my bat on my shoulder.

3 My friends were standing by the fence near the dugout.

4 We were playing on the same team.

Underline the plural nouns in each sentence.

1 My uncles taught me to stand with my feet closer together.

2 The first time I hit a home run, I danced on each of the bases.

3 In the third game, all the players hit the ball.

4 My brothers, sisters, and cousins came to every game.

Circle the singular nouns in each sentence. Underline the plural nouns.

1 The teams and players received awards when the season ended.

2 In the games to come, I will try to be a better hitter, catcher, and teammate.

3 My mother and father were the proudest parents at the assembly.

4 They gave me a new glove for my achievements.

Singular and Plural Nouns

In each sentence below, circle the singular nouns and underline the plural nouns.

1 My homework last night was to write a story about friends.

2 I thought about the people at home who are my friends.

3 My three dogs, one cat, and four birds are also my pals.

4 I wrote about adventures with my pets and my buddies.

Write each noun from the list in the correct column on the chart.
Remember that some nouns keep the same form in the singular and plural.

chair	mice
mouse	chairs
teeth	tooth
sheep	men
foot	feet
man	

	Singular Nouns	Plural Nouns
1	_____	_____
2	_____	_____
3	_____	_____
4	_____	_____
5	_____	_____
6	_____	_____

Write three sentences. Use one singular noun and one plural noun from the chart in each sentence.

1 _____

2 _____

3 _____

Singular and Plural Nouns

Decide if the underlined part of the sentence has an error.
Fill in the bubble next to the correct answer.

1 I read seven <u>chapter in my book</u> last night.
- ○ chapter in my books
- ○ chapters in my book
- ○ correct as is

2 In chapter one, <u>a father and a son</u> went to the mountains.
- ○ a fathers and a son
- ○ a father and a sons
- ○ correct as is

3 They built their campsite under some <u>trees near a creeks</u>.
- ○ tree near a creeks
- ○ trees near a creek
- ○ correct as is

4 The first night, the father saw <u>a bear eating nut</u>.
- ○ a bear eating nuts
- ○ a bears eating nuts
- ○ correct as is

5 Two <u>bear cubs</u> were in the bushes hiding.
- ○ bear cub
- ○ bears cub
- ○ correct as is

6 The <u>bear cubs' mother</u> helped them find berries to eat.
- ○ bear cub's mother
- ○ bear cubs mother
- ○ correct as is

7 In the morning, there were four <u>deers and a sheep</u> nearby.
- ○ deers and a sheeps
- ○ deer and a sheep
- ○ correct as is

8 The <u>son's teeths</u> were red after eating berries.
- ○ son's teeth
- ○ son's tooths
- ○ correct as is

9 Two <u>squirrel ran</u> past Dad's feet and into the tent.
- ○ squirrel rans
- ○ squirrels ran
- ○ correct as is

10 It took almost an hour to get that <u>bird out of the tent's</u>.
- ○ birds out of the tents
- ○ bird out of the tent
- ○ correct as is

Subject and Object Pronouns

A **subject pronoun**—*I, you, he, she, it, we,* or *they*—can replace the subject of a sentence. An **object pronoun**—*me, you, him, her, it, us,* or *them*—can replace a noun that is the object of an action verb or that follows a preposition.

Read the sentences. Circle the subject pronoun in the second sentence that replaces the underlined word or words.

1 The fourth graders read a book about the rain forest.

They read a book about the rain forest.

2 Then, Ada wrote a poem about a huge kapok tree.

Then, she wrote a poem about a huge kapok tree.

3 Juan, Jill, and I painted a mural of rain forest mammals.

We painted a mural of rain forest mammals.

Read the sentences. Draw two lines under the object pronoun in the second sentence that replaces the underlined word or words.

1 Mr. Patel's class sent a fan letter to the author.

Mr. Patel's class sent a letter to her.

2 Ms. Torres, a rain forest expert, visited the fourth graders last week.

Ms. Torres, a rain forest expert, visited them last week.

3 She said, "You can find information in the library."

She said, "You can find it in the library."

Circle the subject pronoun and underline the object pronoun in each sentence.

1 You can call me tonight about our class project.

2 Will he make an informative poster for us?

Subject and Object Pronouns

Choose the pronoun in parentheses ( ) that completes each sentence, and write it on the line. Then, identify the kind of pronoun in the sentence by writing *S* for *subject* or *O* for *object*.

1 _____ took a boat trip through the Everglades. (We, Us) _____

2 The boat's captain gave _____ a special tour. (we, us) _____

3 The captain said, " _____ will love the wildlife here!" (You, Us) _____

4 _____ brought a camera in my backpack. (I, Me) _____

5 I used _____ to photograph birds, turtles, and alligators. (he, it) _____

6 My sister Kit carried paper and pencils with _____ . (she, her) _____

7 Kit used _____ to sketch scenes of the Everglades. (they, them) _____

8 _____ is an excellent artist. (She, Her) _____

Rewrite each sentence. Replace the underlined words with the correct subject or object pronoun.

1 Our grandparents sent a postcard to my sister, my brother, and me.

_____

2 The postcard was addressed to my older brother.

_____

3 My sister gave the toys to Jen and Theo.

_____

Subject and Object Pronouns

Fill in the bubble next to the pronoun that can replace the underlined words.

1 Carlos and Sue have a very popular pet-care service.
○ They
○ Them
○ He

2 Many people hire Carlos and Sue to feed their cats.
○ her
○ they
○ them

3 Carlos asked Jenna and me to help out for a day.
○ we
○ us
○ me

4 Jenna and I were delighted to help.
○ We
○ Us
○ They

Fill in the bubble next to the pronoun that correctly completes each sentence.

1 Dot, Ed, and ___ visited the Air and Space Museum recently.
○ I
○ me
○ us

2 Fortunately, ___ knew his way around the huge exhibition hall.
○ her
○ he
○ him

3 ___ really wanted to see the biplanes.
○ She
○ Them
○ Her

4 Then, Ed told Dot and ___ about the Wright Brothers' flight.
○ I
○ me
○ she

Possessive Pronouns

Underline the possessive pronoun in each sentence.

1 I miss my best friend, Carlos, because he is spending the summer in Seattle, Washington.

2 He is staying with his favorite cousins, Blanca and Eduardo, during July and August.

3 The cousins have been showing Carlos around their city.

4 Blanca also showed Carlos her favorite beach for clam digging.

5 Eduardo said, "Carlos, this will be your best vacation ever!"

6 Then Blanca added, "Our next stop will be the Space Needle."

Write the possessive pronoun from the list that completes each sentence. Use the underlined word or words to help you.

> my   her   his   their   our

1 _____ grandparents, Abuelo and Abuela, sent me a long letter in Spanish.

2 They said that _____ goal was to help me learn the language.

3 Abuela included the words to _____ favorite Spanish song she learned as a child.

4 Abuelo wrote a list of _____ special tips for learning a language.

5 During _____ next visit, we will try to speak as much Spanish as possible.

6 I know that _____ speaking ability will improve with this kind of help.

Possessive Pronouns

Choose the possessive pronoun in parentheses ( ) that correctly completes each sentence. Write it on the line.

1 The sports magazine and newspaper are _____ . (my, mine)

2 Where is _____ atlas of the United States? (your, yours)

3 Which of the mysteries on the shelf is _____ ? (your, yours)

4 These new dictionaries will soon be _____ . (our, ours)

5 Where is _____ copy of *Charlotte's Web*? (her, hers)

Write the possessive pronoun that completes each sentence.

1 My brother and I really enjoy visiting _____ neighborhood library.

2 Every year, Ms. Lee, the librarian, displays _____ choices for the year's best reading.

3 Then, all the library users vote for _____ favorite books, too.

4 For _____ favorite, I chose a photo biography about Babe Ruth.

5 Luke said that _____ first choice was Jerry Spinelli's new novel.

Write two sentences about something you treasure. Use a possessive pronoun in each sentence.

1 _____

_____

2 _____

_____

Possessive Pronouns

Look at the underlined words in each sentence. Fill in the bubble next to the possessive pronoun that refers back to the underlined word or words.

1 <u>I</u> love baseball, and _____ hobby is collecting baseball cards.
- ○ his
- ○ your
- ○ our
- ○ my

2 Many <u>baseball-card collectors</u> buy _____ cards from special dealers.
- ○ your
- ○ his
- ○ their
- ○ her

3 A <u>classmate named Ralph</u> keeps _____ cards in an album.
- ○ my
- ○ his
- ○ our
- ○ your

4 <u>Sue</u> treasures that rare Jackie Robinson card of _____.
- ○ ours
- ○ mine
- ○ hers
- ○ his

5 On Saturday, <u>Mom and I</u> packed _____ lunch and ate it at the ballpark.
- ○ his
- ○ their
- ○ your
- ○ our

6 Once, <u>all the players</u> signed _____ names on a baseball for me.
- ○ his
- ○ their
- ○ my
- ○ her

7 <u>I</u> exclaimed, "This signed baseball is _____ greatest treasure!"
- ○ theirs
- ○ ours
- ○ my
- ○ yours

8 Grandfather asked <u>me</u> whether this new baseball cap was _____.
- ○ her
- ○ you
- ○ your
- ○ mine

9 When the players scored, <u>people in the audience</u> waved _____ baseball caps.
- ○ his
- ○ my
- ○ their
- ○ her

10 I just read a book about <u>Roberto Clemente</u> and _____ amazing career.
- ○ his
- ○ my
- ○ their
- ○ your

Action Verbs

An **action verb** is a word that shows action. Some action verbs, such as *jump*, name actions you can see. Others, such as *think*, name actions you can't see.

Underline the action verb in each sentence, and then write it on the line.

1 Judy Hindley wrote a book about the history of string. _____

2 An illustrator painted funny pictures about string. _____

3 Long ago, people twisted vines into long, strong ropes. _____

4 People still weave long, thin fibers into cloth. _____

5 My sister knits sweaters from thick wool yarn. _____

6 We stretched the rope hammock from tree to tree. _____

Underline the action verb that is more vivid.

1 The rabbit quickly (moved, hopped) across the lawn.

2 I (pounded, touched) the nail with my hammer.

3 The thirsty dog (drank, slurped) the water noisily.

4 I (made, sewed) a quilt from scraps of fabric.

Write three sentences about how someone did something.

1 _____

2 _____

3 _____

Action Verbs

Circle the action verb in each sentence.

1 People use string in many different ways.

2 Fran and I tie the packages with string.

3 We imagine people from earlier times.

4 These people invented rope, string, and cord.

5 The lively, happy tone of this story amazes me.

For each sentence, underline the action verb in parentheses that creates a more vivid picture.

1 We (sit, lounge) on the big chairs near the pool.

2 The horses (go, gallop) across the field.

3 Minna and Max (devour, eat) their sandwiches in a hurry.

4 The workers (drag, move) the heavy load across the yard.

5 Rosa and I (put, staple) the parts together.

 Use each of these action verbs in a sentence: *follow, shout, rush, slip, pound.* Write your sentences on another sheet of paper.

Action Verbs

Fill in the bubble next to the action verb in each sentence.

1 Jake and Paulo practiced together all summer.
- ○ together
- ○ practiced
- ○ all

2 They joined the their school's debate team.
- ○ school's
- ○ joined
- ○ team

3 Their team debated the national champions last week.
- ○ debated
- ○ national
- ○ week

4 The team won the second place in the national debates.
- ○ team
- ○ won
- ○ second

For each sentence, fill in the bubble next to the more vivid action verb.

1 At the beach, we ____ for pieces of driftwood.
- ○ looked
- ○ hunted

2 We ____ into the foamy waves.
- ○ walked
- ○ plunged

3 I ____ my beach towel under a large umbrella.
- ○ put
- ○ spread

4 The wild horses ____ along the sandy seashore.
- ○ galloped
- ○ ran

Verb Tenses and Agreement

Present-tense verbs show action that is happening now or on a regular basis. Present-tense verbs agree in number with who or what is doing the action. **Past-tense verbs** show action that took place in the past. Most past-tense verbs end in -ed. **Future-tense verbs** show action that will happen in the future. The future tense is formed with the verb *will*.

Write *present* if the underlined word is a present-tense verb, *past* if the underlined word is a past-tense verb, and *future* if it is future tense.

1. The story of sneakers <u>started</u> with the development of rubber. _____

2. People in Central and South America <u>melted</u> gum from trees. _____

3. On Friday she <u>will celebrate</u> her tenth birthday. _____

4. Rubber <u>protected</u> the wearer's feet. _____

5. Gum <u>acts</u> as an eraser. _____

6. Everyone <u>will carry</u> a small backpack. _____

7. Unfortunately, pure rubber <u>cracks</u> in cold weather. _____

8. Charles Goodyear <u>developed</u> a solution. _____

9. We <u>will visit</u> two museums. _____

Look at the sentences with present-tense verbs above. Rewrite each one with the past-tense form of the verb.

1. _____

2. _____

Verb Tenses and Agreement

Underline each subject. Decide whether it is singular or plural. Then, circle the present-tense verb that correctly completes the sentence and write it on the line.

1 Anna _____ dark-purple sneakers.   **wear**   **wears**

2 The sneakers _____ a squeaky sound on the floor.   **make**   **makes**

3 The girl _____ her sister how to tie her sneakers.   **teach**   **teaches**

4 Tight sneakers _____ your feet.   **hurt**   **hurts**

5 Loose sneakers _____ blisters.   **cause**   **causes**

6 Joe _____ his new sneakers under his bed.   **place**   **places**

Look at the present-tense verbs in the list. Decide whether they agree in number with a singular or a plural subject. Then, write each word in the correct column in the chart. The first one is done for you.

lace	laces
design	designs
reach	reaches
erase	erases

Present-Tense Verbs	
With Most Singular Subjects and *he, she, it*	**With Plural Subjects and** *I, we, you, they*
laces	lace
_____	_____
_____	_____
_____	_____

Verb Tenses and Agreement

Look at the underlined verb or verbs. Fill in the bubble next to the correct tense.

1 Tomorrow, we <u>will march</u> in the Independence Day parade.
○ past
○ present
○ future

2 Last week, my sister and I <u>sewed</u> our old-fashioned costumes.
○ past
○ present
○ future

3 Everyone <u>participates</u> in the celebration.
○ past
○ present
○ future

4 <u>Will</u> local cowhands <u>ride</u> their horses?
○ past
○ present
○ future

Complete each sentence. Fill in the bubble next to the correct verb tense.

1 Pari _____ in the Thanksgiving day parade every year.
○ march
○ marches
○ will march

2 Next year, she _____ the cornet.
○ play
○ played
○ will play

3 Her parents _____ the parade every year.
○ watch
○ watches
○ will watch

4 Last year, they _____ hot chocolate and blankets to stay warm.
○ bring
○ brings
○ brought

Main and Helping Verbs

Main verbs show the main action in a sentence.
Helping verbs help the main verb show tense. Helping verbs, such as *am, is, are, was, were, has, have, had*, or *will*, work with main verbs to tell when an action occurs.

Read each sentence. Underline the helping verb once and the main verb twice.

1 What will happen to the doughnuts?

2 Uncle Ulysses has installed new lights in the lunchroom.

3 Homer was polishing the metal trimmings.

4 Uncle Ulysses had tinkered with the inside workings.

5 The Ladies' Club was gathering.

6 Homer will handle everything.

7 Mr. Gabby was talking to Homer about his job.

8 A chauffeur had helped a woman out of a black car.

9 Now she is wearing an apron.

10 She will need some nutmeg.

In each sentence, circle the main verb and underline the helping verb. Then, identify when the action occurs by writing *past, present*, or *future*.

1 The lady had asked for baking powder. _____

2 The rings of batter will drop into the hot fat. _____

3 Homer is learning about the doughnut machine. _____

4 People will enjoy the doughnuts later. _____

Main and Helping Verbs

Read each sentence. Underline the main verb. Then, circle the helping verb that correctly completes the sentence, and write it on the line.

1 Justin _____ cooking seafood stew. (will, was)

2 He _____ added spices and lemon juice. (had, is)

3 Sally and Mick _____ prepared stew before. (will, have)

4 Justin _____ tasting the broth. (is, had)

5 His friends _____ just arrived for dinner. (are, have)

Underline the main verbs and write the helping verbs on the lines.

1 On Saturday, Betty will bake rye bread.   _____

2 Henry has pickled some fresh cucumbers.   _____

3 Gertrude is picking raspberries and blackberries.   _____

4 Alison had planted an herb garden.   _____

5 Marie and Harry have tossed the salad.   _____

Write sentences using the main and helping verbs below.

1 will meet _____

_____

2 had arrived _____

_____

Main and Helping Verbs

Decide if the underlined verbs in each sentence are correct.
Then, fill in the bubble next to the correct answer.

1 Today, Francesca <u>will traveled</u> to Peru by plane.
○ is traveling
○ am traveling
○ correct as is

2 She <u>is photograph</u> the stone ruins of Machu Picchu next week.
○ will photograph
○ had photographed
○ correct as is

3 This city <u>was constructed</u> during the reigns of Pachacutec Inca Yupanqui and Túpac Inca Yupanqui.
○ has constructed
○ is constructing
○ correct as is

4 Since then, many people <u>will visited</u> the ruins of the city.
○ have visited
○ have visiting
○ correct as is

5 Yesterday, Francesca's brothers <u>had looking</u> at pictures of Machu Picchu.
○ have looking
○ were looking
○ correct as is

6 They <u>were wondering</u> about the Inca civilization.
○ had wondering
○ has wonder
○ correct as is

7 Centuries ago, the Inca <u>had creating</u> a great empire.
○ have creating
○ had created
○ correct as is

8 What <u>had happening</u> to them?
○ has happening
○ had happened
○ correct as is

9 The Spanish explorers <u>will conquered</u> the Inca in 1532.
○ had conquered
○ are conquered
○ correct as is

10 Francesca <u>will learn</u> about Inca culture in present-day Peru.
○ has learning
○ was learned
○ correct as is

Linking Verbs

Underline the linking verb in each sentence and circle the main words it links.

A **linking verb** links the subject of a sentence to other words in the sentence. A linking verb does not show action. It tells what the subject is, was, or will be.

1 I am an enthusiastic reader.

2 My favorite books are nonfiction.

3 This bookstore is the best one in town.

4 The nonfiction books here are always interesting.

5 The store's owner is very knowledgeable.

6 His name is Terry Baldes.

7 Mr. Baldes was once an inventor and a scientist.

8 Last Saturday's main event was an appearance by my favorite author.

Write the linking verb in each sentence on the line.

1 An important invention is the telephone. _____

2 The telephone's inventor was Alexander Graham Bell. _____

3 At one time, most telephones were black. _____

4 Cell phones were uncommon 30 years ago. _____

Write two sentences. Include a linking verb in each one.

1 _____

2 _____

Linking Verbs

Underline the correct linking verb in ( ) .
Write *S* if the subject is singular and *P* if it is plural.

1 The natural history museum (was, were) busy last weekend. _____

2 Many visitors (was, were) tourists. _____

3 The new displays of rocks and gems (is, are) very popular. _____

4 The museum's first floor (is, are) full of Native American artifacts. _____

5 The carved wooden canoes (is, are) enormous. _____

6 The Tlingit woodcarvers (was, were) true artists. _____

7 This canoe (was, were) hand-painted over a hundred years ago. _____

8 I (am, is) a big supporter of the museum. _____

Complete each sentence. Write *is* or *are* on the line.

1 The apatasaurus skeleton _____ gigantic.

2 The exhibit cards _____ very informative.

3 The tiny dinosaur _____ really cute.

Write a sentence with a singular subject and a sentence with a plural subject.
Include a linking verb in each sentence.

1 _____

2 _____

Linking Verbs

Read each sentence below. Then, fill in the bubble next to the linking verb that correctly completes the sentence.

1 Denver, Colorado, _____ a large city.
- ○ were
- ○ are
- ○ is

2 This growing metropolis _____ a mile high.
- ○ are
- ○ is
- ○ were

3 Gold prospectors _____ the city's founders in 1858.
- ○ is
- ○ was
- ○ were

4 From 1860 to 1945, Denver _____ a mining and agricultural community.
- ○ were
- ○ was
- ○ will be

5 Today, many local residents _____ government workers.
- ○ are
- ○ is
- ○ was

6 Now, the automobile _____ the quickest way to travel.
- ○ were
- ○ is
- ○ are

7 In earlier times, horses and buggies _____ popular modes of transportation.
- ○ were
- ○ is
- ○ was

8 I _____ a student in a Denver public school.
- ○ were
- ○ am
- ○ is

9 Last year, my school's sports teams _____ very successful.
- ○ was
- ○ were
- ○ is

10 I _____ a spectator at the local games.
- ○ was
- ○ were
- ○ is

Irregular Verbs

Underline the irregular verb in each sentence.

1 This morning, Mom bought red and green toothbrushes.

2 Pat made a tuna sandwich in the kitchen.

3 Mom quickly came into the dining room.

4 Chris rode her bicycle over to Pat's house.

5 Chris shook her head in great amusement.

6 They heard a great deal of noise in the kitchen.

7 Chris took a close look at the bright red toothbrush.

8 Pat carefully thought about the green and red toothbrushes.

9 Chris broke the silence with a sly laugh.

Circle the irregular past-tense verb in parentheses ( ). Then, write it on the line to complete the sentence.

1 We _____ a funny story about two toothbrushes. (hear, heard)

2 Pat _____ his decision after 15 long minutes. (made, make)

3 Mom finally _____ EJ an orange toothbrush. (buy, bought)

4 EJ _____ into a song with a big smile on his face. (broke, break)

5 We all _____ to the nearest supermarket on our bikes. (ride, rode)

6 Chris _____ to the store with us. (came, come)

Irregular Verbs

Underline the helping verb and the irregular past participle in each sentence.

An **irregular verb** does not form the past tense by adding *-ed*. The past participle is the form of the verb used with the helping verbs *has, have, had,* or *will have.*

1 We have chosen a fantastic day for our school picnic.

2 Mr. Torres has brought all the food and beverages in his van.

3 We have eaten all of the carrots on the table.

4 Ms. Chang has hidden the prizes for the treasure hunt.

5 By noon, our teacher had taken over 40 photographs.

6 All the fourth graders have gone on a short walk to the lake.

7 They had heard about the great paddleboats there.

8 Some of my friends have ridden in the boats.

Circle the irregular past participle in parentheses ( ). Then, write it on the line to complete the sentence.

1 By May, I had _____ about an amazing automobile. (hear, heard)

2 Test drivers have _____ it on experimental runs. (taken, took)

3 My friend's family has _____ to Utah to see it. (went, gone)

4 My friend has _____ in the automobile, too. (ridden, rode)

5 I have _____ this car as a research topic. (chose, chosen)

6 My mom has _____ photos of the car, too. (bought, buy)

Irregular Verbs

Complete each sentence. Fill in the bubble next to the irregular past-tense verb.

1 Last week, we ____ the news about our baseball team's victory.
○ hear
○ heard
○ hears

2 Yesterday morning, Mom and I ____ the bus downtown.
○ rode
○ rides
○ ride

3 Then, we ____ in line for an hour.
○ stand
○ stands
○ stood

4 We finally ____ four tickets to the first game in the playoffs.
○ bought
○ buys
○ buying

Complete each sentence. Fill in the bubble next to the correct helping verb and past participle.

1 That old adobe house ____ on top of the mesa for a century.
○ has stood
○ has stand
○ has stands

2 We ____ up there many times.
○ have rode
○ have ride
○ have ridden

3 Our great-grandfather ____ pictures of the house long ago.
○ had drawn
○ had draw
○ had drew

4 We ____ the sketches for many years.
○ have keep
○ have kept
○ have keeps

Adjectives

An **adjective** is a word that tells more about a person, place, animal, or thing.

In the following sentences, circle the adjectives that tell what kind. Underline the adjectives that tell how many.

1 We watched many colorful creatures swim through the dark water.

2 A few tilefish were building small burrows.

3 Suddenly, one strange and unusual fish swam by us.

4 Eugenie swam over to the mysterious fish.

5 It looked like a jawfish with a big head and four dark patches on its back.

6 Was this rare fish a new species?

7 We put the tiny fish in a large bucket of cold seawater.

8 Eugenie has made several fun and interesting discoveries.

Complete each sentence with an adjective that tells what kind or how many.

1 The _____ fish was named after David.

2 The fish lived in a _____ burrow at the bottom of the ocean.

3 David took _____ photographs that appeared in magazines.

Write two sentences. Use adjectives that tell what kind and how many in each sentence.

1 _____

2 _____

Adjectives

Write an adjective to complete each sentence.

1 The _____ dog ate most of the cat's food.

2 The _____ cat found a nearly empty bowl.

3 The cat ate what remained of her _____ meal.

4 The cat pushed the _____ dish over to where a

_____ girl was sitting.

5 The girl refilled the dish with _____ food.

Read each sentence. Circle the adjective that describes each underlined noun.

1 The orange <u>cat</u> saw the shaggy <u>dog</u> sitting in the dark <u>corner</u>.

2 The cat saw some <u>cat food</u> on the dog's droopy <u>mouth</u>.

3 The cat slipped out of the little <u>kitchen</u> and went into the quiet <u>backyard</u>.

4 She started digging in the soft <u>dirt</u> under a shady <u>tree</u>.

5 The dog looked out the enormous <u>window</u> and saw the cat with a large <u>bone</u>.

Write two sentences that tell what happened next. Use vivid adjectives in your writing.

1 _____

_____

2 _____

_____

Adjectives

Fill in the bubble next to the word in each sentence that is an adjective.

1 I had an important decision to make this morning.
- ○ important
- ○ decision
- ○ morning

2 I wanted to buy an appropriate pet for my sister.
- ○ wanted
- ○ buy
- ○ appropriate

3 First, I looked at a striped lizard.
- ○ First
- ○ striped
- ○ lizard

4 Then, I considered getting two hamsters.
- ○ considered
- ○ two
- ○ hamsters

5 The white hamster was named George.
- ○ white
- ○ hamster
- ○ George

6 I admired the noisy parrot.
- ○ I
- ○ noisy
- ○ parrot

7 I watched a gigantic turtle on a rock.
- ○ gigantic
- ○ turtle
- ○ rock

8 Several gerbils ran on a wheel.
- ○ Several
- ○ gerbils
- ○ wheel

9 I finally decided to get a saltwater aquarium.
- ○ decided
- ○ saltwater
- ○ aquarium

10 I'm sure my family will enjoy the colorful fish.
- ○ sure
- ○ family
- ○ colorful

ANSWER KEY

Page 5
1. declarative 2. imperative
3. exclamatory 4. interrogative
1. incomplete 2. complete
3. complete 4. incomplete
5. complete
Action words will vary. Possible
answers: 1. Sarah stood at the edge of
the square. 2. The sword slid out of the
stone.

Page 6
1. ?, interrogative 2. !, exclamatory
3. ., imperative 4. ., declarative
Verbs will vary. Possible answers:
1. listened, declarative 2. play,
interrogative 3. pass, imperative
4. won, exclamatory
Sentences will vary.

Page 7
3, 5, and 7 are correct as is.
1. Do you like 2. the Middle Ages.
4. your life? 6. in the ocean!
8. Tell me another story
9. the Caribbean Sea! 10. his trip.

Page 8
1. A small family | lived on a faraway
planet.
2. The family's two children | played
near the space launch.
3. The little girl | dreamed about life on
Earth.
4. Huge spaceships | landed daily on
the planet.
1. The planet's inhabitants | lived in
underground homes.
2. A special machine | manufactures air
inside the family's home.
3. Many toys and games | cluttered the
children's playroom.
4. The children's father | described
weather on Earth.
1. The underground home contained
large, comfortable rooms.
2. The playful child rolled his clay
into a ball.

Page 9
1. My whole family
2. The warm, sunny day
3. My cousin Fred 4. Everyone
1. watched the space shuttle on TV
this morning.
2. rocketed into space at 6:00 A.M.
3. released a satellite into space.
4. landed smoothly on Monday at noon.
Sentences will vary.

Page 10
1. complete subject 2. complete
predicate 3. simple subject
4. complete predicate 5. complete
subject 6. simple predicate
7. simple subject 8. simple predicate
9. complete subject
10. complete predicate

Page 11
1. bears, rabbits, and pigs
2. Carrots, beets, and squash
3. Teddy and Osito
4. brothers and sisters
1. cleaned and peeled 2. laughed and
giggled 3. waited and watched
4. weeds and waters
5. writes and edits
1. buys and reads, CP
2. authors and illustrators, CS

Page 12
1. teacher, students
The teacher and her students visited
the ocean.
2. Seagulls, Pelicans
Seagulls and pelicans flew overhead.
3. Carlos, Tanya
Carlos and Tanya ran on the beach.
4. Seashells, Seaweed
Seashells and seaweed littered the
sand.
1. paints, draws
The artist paints and draws sea life.
2. collect, decorate
I collect and decorate driftwood.
3. swim, dive
Seals swim and dive near the pier.

Page 13
1. deer and bison 2. Rosa and Kay
3. students and teachers 4. friends and I
1. moaned and howled 2. picked and
peeled 3. wrote and revised
4. cut and polished

Page 14
1. simple 2. compound 3. compound
4. simple 5. simple
1. Connor had seen many parks in his
life, but he never had seen a park like
this one. 2. Dad brought a pair of
binoculars, and Nate used them to look
for animals. 3. He saw his first live
bear, and the hair stood up on his
arms. 4. It was an exciting moment,
but it only lasted a second. 5. The bear
was no bear at all, and Nate was
embarrassed. 6. He hadn't seen a
bear, but he kept looking.

Page 15
1. One day we were in the park, and
we saw two ducks swimming by.
2. We watched the ducks for a while,
but they disappeared into the tall
grass. 3. The ducks might have gone to
a nest, or they could have swum to the
shore. 4. We walked along the grassy
bank, but we could not find them
anywhere. 5. We sat down on the
dock, and out came the ducks again.
1. but 2. but 3. and 4. and 5. or
Sentences will vary.

Page 16
1. compound 2. compound
3. simple 4. compound
1. correct as is 2. the sun, and
some stars 3. the sun, but they are
4. blue light, or do they

Page 17
1. farmer, house, road 2. farmer,
wheat, soybeans, corn 3. fields, crop
4. crops, rows 5. plants, farmer,
weeds, bugs
1. John Vasquez, Tulsa, Oklahoma
2. Vasquez Farm, Rising J Horse Ranch
3. Mr. Vasquez, Sally 4. Joker
5. October, Vasquez Farm,
Harvest Celebration
Sample sentences: 1. We walked down
Oak Street to Blair Park.
2. My Aunt Ellen lives in Denver.

Page 18
1. story, celebrations Atlanta
Constitution 2. movie, poodles
Three Dogs on a Summer Night
3. campfire "She'll Be Comin'
'Round the Mountain"
4. friend, grandparents August, John,
Germany 5. family, beach Memorial
Day **Common nouns:** newspaper, day,
magazine, city, book, month, park
Proper nouns: *The Sun News*, July,
Harry Potter, Yellowstone National
Park, *National Geographic*, Tuesday,
Chicago
Common and proper nouns will vary.

Page 19
2, 4, 6, and 8 are correct as is.
1. Abraham Lincoln School 3. "Row,
Row, Row Your Boat" 5. *Hello,
Universe* 7. Spanish class begins at
noon 9. about Washington, D.C.
10. Austin's Better Books

Page 20
1. door, cap, bat, game 2. bat, shoulder 3. fence, dugout 4. team
1. uncles, feet 2. bases 3. players
4. brothers, sisters, cousins
1. (season), teams, players, awards
2. (hitter), (catcher), (teammate), games
3. (mother), (father), (assembly), parents
4. (glove), achievements

Page 21
1. (homework), (night), (story), friends
2. (home), people, friends
3. (cat), dogs, birds, pals
4. adventures, pets, buddies
Singular nouns: 1. chair 2. mouse
3. tooth 4. sheep 5. foot 6. man
Plural nouns: 1. chairs 2. mice
3. teeth 4. sheep 5. feet 6. men
Sentences will vary.

Page 22
2, 5, and 6 are correct as is.
1. chapters in my book 3. trees near a creek 4. a bear eating nuts 7. deer and a sheep 8. son's teeth 9. squirrels ran 10. bird out of the tent

Page 23
1. they 2. she 3. we
1. her 2. them 3. it
1. (You), me 2. (he), us

Page 24
1. We, S 2. us, O 3. You, S 4. I, S
5. it, O 6. her, O 7. them, O 8. She, S
1. They sent a postcard to us.
2. It was addressed to him.
3. She gave the toys to them.

Page 25
1. They 2. them 3. us 4. We
1. I 2. he 3. She 4. me

Page 26
1. my 2. his 3. their 4. her
5. your 6. Our
1. My 2. their 3. her 4. his
5. our 6. my

Page 27
1. mine 2. your 3. yours
4. ours 5. her
1. our 2. her 3. their 4. my 5. his
Sentences will vary.

Page 28
1. my 2. their 3. his 4. hers 5. our
6. their 7. my 8. mine 9. their 10. his

Page 29
1. wrote 2. painted 3. twisted
4. weave 5. knits 6. stretched
1. hopped 2. pounded

3. slurped 4. sewed
Sentences will vary.

Page 30
1. use 2. tie 3. imagine
4. invented 5. amazes
1. lounge 2. gallop 3. devour
4. drag 5. staple

Page 31
1. practiced 2. joined
3. debated 4. won
1. hunted 2. plunged 3. spread
4. galloped

Page 32
1. past 2. past 3. future 4. past
5. present 6. future 7. present
8. past 9. future
1. Gum acted as an eraser.
2. Unfortunately, pure rubber cracked in cold weather.

Page 33
1. Anna, wears 2. sneakers, make
3. girl, teaches 4. sneakers, hurt
5. sneakers, cause 6. Joe, places
With Most Singular subjects: laces, designs, reaches, erases
With Plural Subjects: lace, design, reach, erase

Page 34
1. future 2. past 3. present 4. future
1. marches 2. will play 3. watch
4. brought

Page 35
1. will happen 2. has installed
3. was polishing 4. had tinkered
5. was gathering 6. will handle
7. was talking 8. had helped
9. is wearing 10. will need
1. had (asked), past 2. will (drop), future 3. is (learning), present
4. will (enjoy), future

Page 36
1. was cooking 2. had added
3. have prepared 4. is tasting
5. have arrived
1. will bake 2. has pickled 3. is picking
4. had planted 5. have tossed
Sentences will vary.

Page 37
3, 6, and 10 are correct as is.
1. is traveling 2. will photograph
4. have visited 5. were looking
7. had created 8. had happened
9. had conquered

Page 38
1. (I) am (reader) 2. (books) are (nonfiction) 3. (bookstore) is (one)

4. (books) are (interesting)
5. (owner) is (knowledgeable)
6. (name) is (Terry Baldes)
7. (Mr. Baldes) was (inventor, scientist)
8. (event) was (appearance)
1. is 2. was 3. were 4. were
Sentences will vary.

Page 39
1. was, S 2. were, P 3. are, P 4. is, S
5. are, P 6. were, P 7. was, S 8. am, S
1. is 2. are 3. is
Sentences will vary.

Page 40
1. is 2. is 3. were 4. was 5. are
6. is 7. were 8. am 9. were 10. was

Page 41
1. bought 2. made 3. came
4. rode 5. shook 6. heard
7. took 8. thought 9. broke
1. heard 2. made 3. bought
4. broke 5. rode 6. came

Page 42
1. have chosen 2. has brought
3. have eaten 4. has hidden
5. had taken 6. have gone
7. had heard 8. have ridden
1. heard 2. taken 3. gone
4. ridden 5. chosen 6. bought

Page 43
1. heard 2. rode 3. stood 4. bought
1. has stood 2. have ridden
3. had drawn 4. have kept

Page 44
1. (colorful), (dark) many 2. (small) few
3. (strange), (unusual) one
4. (mysterious) 5. (big), (dark) four
6. (rare), (new) 7. (tiny), (large), (cold)
8. (fun), (interesting) several
Sample answers:
1. small, mysterious 2. sandy, small, long 3. underwater, several, many
Sentences will vary.

Page 45
Sample answers:
1. big, hungry 2. fuzzy, brown, little
3. missing, tasty 4. metal, silver; red-headed, young 5. more, tasty, good
1. orange, shaggy, dark 2. some, droopy 3. little, quiet 4. soft, shady
5. enormous, large
Sentences will vary.

Page 46
1. important 2. appropriate 3. striped
4. two 5. white 6. noisy 7. gigantic
8. Several 9. saltwater 10. colorful